GAMING THE REAPER

—◆—

How to Win at Life and Optimize the
Sh#t Out of Your own Potential

Zack Kowalske

Copyright © 2023 by Zack Kowalske

All rights reserved.

No portion of this book may be reproduced in any form without written permission from the publisher or author, except as permitted by U.S. copyright law.

For Jennifer and Brooklynn, thank you for putting up with me and my many eccentric dreams.
And to David, Top This.

Contents

Introduction — VI

1. Part 1 — 1
   Common Traits of Great Achievers
2. Part 2 — 10
   Habits that Hinder High Achievement
3. Part 3 — 16
   Ten Daily Behaviors of High Achievers
4. Conclusion — 39

Afterword — 41

About Author — 42

INTRODUCTION

You're going to die. While this statement is fact, at least as of this writing, death should really be treated as a non-answer, a mathematical constant; if you dwell too long it just becomes depressing. Therefore, contemplating it serves no true value other than to provide a driving force. I am still banking on uploading my conscious into a robot overlord or my alchemy skills having an unexpected breakthrough in the garage. Congratulations! The fact that you're reading this book means you are currently winning the foot race against the Reaper and that you would like to enter the cheat code for the rest of the game (Up, Down, Up, Down,A,B,A,B). I am often asked, "how do you have the time?," the answer is simple because I have the drive. As a Crime Scene Detective, I often interact with how we all end the game. Consequently, I want to maximize the value I get out of it. I want to eat the metaphorical mushroom and level up. At this point, if you are reading this book then you know that you can do a little bit more to optimize. Good for you on your honest self-reflection. That's not to say you don't work hard, but you can do more...being brutally honest with yourself is one of the biggest aspects to achieving true personal success.

It's time to level up and go on a quest.

Do you put in the extra hours and make the effort to go above and beyond? Do you consider yourself motivated and driven? Do you try to stay organized, manage your time, schedule diligently; yet you are stagnant?

You feel frustrated because you just know that you can do better. For some reason, all your efforts are not achieving the spectacular successes that you envisioned. In fact, you often feel stuck in place and fighting a losing battle.

You often look at high achievers with envy and wonder what their secret is (yep totally looking at you Elon). What is it that allows them to skyrocket ahead and in a manner that appears effortless? How do they manage to leap from one spectacular success to the next? What makes them stand out and shine at whatever they do?

What's the secret?

What do super-achievers have that you don't? The short answer is...nothing! High achievement is not a product of luck, nor is it an innate quality that some people possess. Anybody can become a high achiever wherever they are in life and whatever their personal goals may be. Becoming a high achiever simply means attaining your personal greatness. Arete is a Greek word meaning to display the full realization of potential or function of a person or thing, or to *be the best version of one's self.*

Like any skill that needs to be learned and honed, high achievement can become an acquired trait. That's right, becoming a high achiever is totally within your reach through the cultivation of several habits that you put to action.

What you'll get from this book.

First, you'll get a quick rundown of the common traits and qualities of high achievers. You'll be able to assess yourself against those concepts, determine where you are and where you want to be, and design your personal treasure map where X marks the spot. The goal is to redefine your mindset into making every day your harlot (the MS Word Paperclip informed me my other choice of word was offensive). More importantly, you'll begin to recognize the emergence of these traits in yourself as you begin to practice your daily habits. Developing good habits starts with recognizing the negative habits you need to break. Within this text you'll get a brief rundown on habits that could be sabotaging your ability to become your best version. It was not until I quit smoking, drinking, and prioritized my sleep health that I kicked into the next level of my own personal growth. Personal evolution and discipline is a continuous cycle. For me, regular exercise is my personal next step; I just hate the idea of it, we all have room to grow.

Finally, this book will walk you through 10 powerful habits common to all high achievers. Most of them are simple, and some of them may actually surprise you because they're so mundane. While each of the practices is highly effective on its own, putting all of the traits into action together will compound the effects to bring about a remarkable transformation in how you go about setting objectives, mindset to purpose, and achieving goals. These habits feed off and feed into each other so that their combined results will craft you into the best version of yourself; they have for me.

PART 1

COMMON TRAITS OF GREAT ACHIEVERS

We all know a great achiever when we see one. For one, they make all the underachievers stand out like a sore thumb and make you question all your life decisions. Have you ever paused to notice the special characteristics that they consistently display? Here are a number of these common traits and mindsets. You may be able to recognize some of them in yourself already, which means you're off to a good start. Otherwise, you can anticipate developing these defining characteristics as you gradually transform into a successful highflier.

They're Action-Oriented

High achievers are doers: inaction, procrastination, and delay are dirty words to them. They're just not part of their mindset. The idea of doing nothing legitimately makes me uncomfortable. That's not to say that I cannot relax on a beach while listening to the waves, but I will be allowing my mind to purposefully wander with development of new projects and goals being the target. The concept of just sitting on the couch mindlessly watching the trending show or never-ending scrolling is not in the playbook. "But Zack that's how I relax from a long day," to which my reply will be that's fine but you will never reach your full potential because you have not accepted the key step: changing your mindset. Maximize every minute, be goal oriented in some way. If you watch an hour normally, try watching only half an hour and then reading a new book or planning out your actionable goals. *Permanent changes happen consciously and slowly.* There is no quick fix and you have to put in the work.

Change your mindset by killing the metaphorical television set.

High achievers roll up their sleeves and get things done. They don't overload themselves with information or spend hours in detailed planning. They've learned not to fear taking risks and usually take action with minimal planning. In a nutshell, inaction is simply not an option regardless of the situation.

They Have Clutter-Free Lives

High achievers are well-organized because they take care to keep their lives clutter-free. Their homes, workspaces, even their cars and garages are typically tidy, streamlined, and free of superfluous clutter. They keep on hand only the essentials they use on a daily basis. There is truth to the less is more concept. If your don't believe me, take the next ten minutes and just web search the "less is more" principal. Tim Ferriss discusses this concept in detail in *The 4-Hour Workweek.*

A clutter-free life goes beyond the mere physical. It gives high achievers amazing mental clarity, focus, and peace of mind. Those with unwavering purpose do not have time for the superfluous or unnecessary personal drama. This is just noise that obscures the path. Surround yourself with those who are supportive or emotionally beneficial. If you have a relationship that exhibits any form of negativity or distraction, then Snoop Dog it and drop it like it's hot. One of the most personally liberating improvements I made in my life was coming to the understanding that I was reliant upon nobody and needed no one's approval. If I don't like you for whatever reason I do not waste my time pretending to be nice, I simply just choose not to engage or involve with you. Think of this as the 80/20 rule to personal relationships, in that 80% of your baggage derives from 20% or your relationships. So cut the fat and move on, your personal profit will dramatically increase.

In other words, physical decluttering declutters the mind as well.

They Take Charge

High achievers make great leaders and managers; their proactive mindset drives them to leap up and take charge when decisive action is needed. They do this naturally without the intention of offending or showing off because others recognize this, they're more than happy to follow.

This quality serves them well in crisis situations and team management. During my career as a Detective and Police Officer, I have found myself in many critical incidents that were fast paced, dangerous, and rapidly changing. Taking charge by making a decision is the quickest way to have a successful outcome and bring order to chaos. Take charge and pick a direction, then start going regardless of obstacles you encounter along the way.

They Thrive on Challenges and Crises

Difficult projects, tight deadlines, setbacks, and crises are exciting challenges for high achievers. Where others may panic or hesitate, a high achiever will usually jump in and save the day.

Failure is a very slim option for high achievers and therefore, they see difficulties as an opportunity for learning and gaining experience. Tough situations are challenging tests of their resilience, persistence, and capabilities.

They're Outcome-Oriented

High achievers are decidedly focused on the outcomes of their actions. When working on a project or task, they regularly stop and assess whether their actions are leading them towards the desired outcome.

Where others may stick blindly to a prior plan or schedule, a high achiever will not hesitate to stop and change actions or goals if they're not aligning to the outcome. Don't be afraid to question why you are doing a task in the manner you are. This just improves the methodology that increases efficacy. At the same time, do not belabor over the process to the point of inefficacy; indecision is just self-imposed inaction.

They're Highly Optimistic

Life for a high achiever never ceases to be a thrilling, exciting adventure to be explored and enjoyed to its fullest. They have immense gratitude but also acceptance. A high achiever understands that life has its ups and downs. They celebrate the good times with gratitude and joy. They face the bad times with acceptance, resilience, and a fierce determination to overcome them.

This outlook is a foolproof recipe for eternal optimism and hope which fuels purpose and passion. This skill alone is one of the most important. Walt Disney built one of the largest multimedia empires of mankind's history. A company that has had a global impact on our cultural evolution, and it started with failure, however he chose to remain optimistic. Pessimism serves no purpose other than self-pity, there are no buildings named after naysayers. On the other hand is the optimist. An optimist is memorable, because they inspire the concept of *"what if?"* and the challenge to the status quo of what is possible.

They're Great Listeners

A high achiever rarely needs to be told what to do twice. That's because they're great listeners. They make sure they've heard and understood all the details and don't hesitate to ask pertinent questions. Naturally, this allows them to get things right the first time around, saving themselves and others a lot of time and frustration.

The bottom line: Observe the high achievers in your workplace or circle of acquaintances and notice how they display these characteristics. You'll almost always find that they do. Do case studies on those that changed an industry or had a significant impact on humanity. You will find that almost everyone of them exhibited a combination of these traits. I have read and watched just about every biography and documentary on Walt Disney, Elon Musk, Albert Einstein, and Theodore Roosevelt because they are my personal role models that have had some sort of impact I desire to replicate. We all learn from teachers, who are yours?

Study those you admire and surround yourself with those who inspire you.

Do you recognize any of these qualities in yourself? If you don't, no worries, they're going to gradually become part of your nature when you begin developing the habits of a high achiever. Remember, high achievers weren't born with these qualities. They're a result of consistent practice and the unique mindset that you will refine over time. They're the core qualities that reflect your personal greatness.

PART 2

HABITS THAT HINDER HIGH ACHIEVEMENT

There are several key habits that are guaranteed to sabotage high achievement and success. This chapter will help you recognize them and identify them in your own behaviors. This information is just for your reference. You don't need to go about actively breaking these habits before beginning your journey, but you should be aware of the dragons that lurk in the forest. As your brain rewires itself and begins to adopt more productive traits, the old ones will gradually be phased out and disappear. However, it's helpful to stay alert for these achievement-hindering habits, that way when you catch yourself practicing them, you can quickly and firmly stop and do the opposite.

Procrastination

"I'll do it tomorrow... I need some time to think this over... the timing's not right... the world won't end if I postpone this for a bit..." These thoughts are all too familiar to all of us. They're the typical excuses we make when we choose inaction over action. As you learned from the previous chapter, procrastination doesn't exist in a high achiever's vocabulary. Likewise, it needs to be deleted from yours. Whenever you start procrastinating stop immediately and act on what you're procrastinating about. Even just planning what you're going to do and taking the first step on a given task will motivate you to keep going. You can even schedule a task and stick to your schedule. Just don't put it off indefinitely.

Seeking Approval

Struggling to gain the approval of others can really derail you on your journey to personal greatness. When your goal is to gain approval, you become more approval-focused rather than outcome-focused. Always do what satisfies you and fulfills your needs and goals first. Never compromise your personal values in exchange for anyone's approval.

Your success will be bittersweet because you know you've sold yourself out. Finally, let your successes and achievements speak for themselves. Do things on your own terms. If others are critical or not happy about it, that's their problem.

Self-Doubt

Self-doubt and negative personal outlook can cripple you. You become fearful of taking risks, thinking outside of the box, and seeking new opportunities. Self-deprecation is a fatal behavior that will erode motivation and optimism.

Be alert to your own negative self-talk and immediately kill it with a mental flame-thrower by internally listing all your unique skills and all of the reasons why you can (and will) succeed.

GAMING THE REAPER 13

Torch the monster of self doubt. You've got this.

Comparing Yourself to Others

Having role models who inspire you is a critical component of self-motivation and growth. You should seek to emulate them. However, personify within your own capacity and take from them what works for you. Comparing yourself to role models or anyone else is an extremely negative practice. Drawing direct comparisons between yourself and people who are more successful, physically fit, financially wealthy, or whatever other desired trait can breed toxic emotions and cause your self-confidence to plummet. Not to mention that the subjective equation will never be balanced in your favor.

In contrast (and just as dangerous), comparing yourself to those who are less successful, less popular, or less wealthy leads to feelings of superiority. This is an equally toxic emotion that weakens your competitiveness and ambition. When you catch yourself making these comparisons, simply stop and give yourself a mental bitch slap and know that you are better than that.

In a nutshell, you are who you are. You are shaped by a myriad of experiences and factors that make you unique to everyone else on the planet. Self-acceptance allows you to soar by harnessing your unique capabilities but also be sure to accept your limitations. As a parent, this is the one trait that I strive to teach my daughter. She is wonderfully perfect at being herself. This is a brilliant balance that high achievers are able to maintain. They never wish to be anyone other than who they are.

Seeking Perfection

If you're a chronic perfectionist, it's unlikely that you'll become a high achiever. This may come as a surprise because it seems logical to associate high achievement with perfectionism. High achievers understand that perfection is unattainable. Therefore, they don't insist on it. That doesn't mean they don't deliver outstanding results. They give it their best and move on.

The bottom line: Do you practice any of these habits in your own life? Hopefully, you're now aware of how they're hindering your progress and holding you back from achieving greatness. Simply note them on your map as "Here Be Dragons" and don't beat yourself up about them. Very soon, you're going to replace them with ones that really work.

Olaus Magnus's Carta marina of 1539, this image is from the 1572 edition. (National Library of Sweden)

PART 3

TEN DAILY BEHAVIORS OF HIGH ACHIEVERS

Ready to change your life? Without further ado, here are ten traits that will rock your world and will bring about that change.

1. Have a crystal-clear vision and keep it alive

Vision brings purpose and meaning into your life. This is why all high achievers are great visionaries. Some dream big, others have modest dreams, but their clear vision is always their primary motivator. It is the blueprint that you calibrate every action and decision against. Vision gives direction to your life and motivates you to rally your efforts and energies towards that specific goal or destination. Having a clear vision keeps you fired up, optimistic, and determined to overcome any obstacle that comes between you and your dream.

Amazingly, this passion and drive extend to all that you do, even if it's not related to your vision. In other words, by clearly defining your vision and keeping it top of mind, you're sowing the first seeds of high achievement.

How do you clearly define your vision? First, you need to put it in writing to bring it to life and make it more tangible for you to consciously process. Write one or two brief sentences describing your current dream...

"My dream is to grow my local business into a global brand..."

"My dream is to retire early and run my own miniature horse farm..."

"My vision is to become the leading expert in my field..."

"My vision is to raise wonderful, successful, happy kids..."

These are a few examples of how to record your vision. It doesn't have to be earth shattering or deserving of a Nobel (totally on my actual list). Your vision reflects your personal passion. The thing or things that make your life meaningful and give you purpose. Now notice that

I wrote "brief sentences describing your current dream". Most high achievers have multiple life goals, dreams, and obsessions; do not limit yourself.

Any vision, grand or miniature.

Daily practice: Once you've identified your vision, you need to keep it alive. Here are two ways to accomplish this:

1. Do one thing every day that brings you closer to realizing your vision. In a nutshell, keep your vision alive and present. Even if you're unable to pursue it full-time in your current job or situation. Read a chapter of a book, listen to a podcast, learn a new skill, or hone a current skill. Just take one action related to your vision every single day.

2. Visualize your dream for a few minutes each day by closing your eyes and imagining that you've already achieved it. Create vivid mental scenarios of what your

life will be like and allow the positive emotions to fill you with joy and hope. This form of meditation could actually alter your brain chemistry and hormone output for the better. By visualizing the positive goals, the body decreases cortisol levels and increases serotonin production, leading to a more happy and focused behavior.

2. Become a problem-solver and troubleshooter

If you want to see a super achiever in action, tell them that something can't be done. That's all they need to hear in order to jump in with both feet and find a way to get it done! As discussed earlier, a high achiever thrives on challenges and problem-solving. They also view it (very wisely) as an opportunity for growth and learning.

Now, most of us don't welcome problems with open arms or actively seek them out. How often have you let out a sigh of relief when somebody else was tasked with some monster of a problem project? When you become a high achiever, you'll not only volunteer but feel insulted if you're turned down.

Daily practice: This habit is easy to develop - just actively seek out problems and find effective ways to resolve them. Don't worry, it gets easier (and more fun) with practice. I had no idea how to fix plumbing or rewire electrical sockets until I became a home owner and started attending the University of Youtube. Now there's not a project in the house I am not capable of accomplishing. I just may choose to hire a professional so that I can devote that time to accomplishing one of my more strategic goals.

Here are some useful problem solving tips to help you get started:

- Consider multiple solutions then narrow them down to the most practical one.

- Do your research.

- Ask an expert for advice.

- Find out why the problem happened. This could give you clues as to what needs to be done to resolve it. Consider this a root cause analysis.

- Draw on prior experiences where you faced a similar issue and recall how it was resolved.

- Think out of the box. Sometimes, the most off the wall solution could be the one that works. A change of perspective is often the solution.

- Don't back down. Persistence is a key characteristic of a high achieving individual. Keep trying and building until you achieve sweet success.

Foster this habit even further by looking for more innovative ways to get things done efficiently. Explore new software and apps that may help you to better delegate, manage teams, or organize your time.

3. Accept full responsibility for your actions

Super achievers are notable for their strong personal discipline. This includes their willingness to take full responsibility for their actions. Taking responsibility basically means holding yourself accountable for the outcomes you initiate, both the good and the bad. One of the best descriptions of incorporating this mindset is the pivotal book *Extreme Ownership: How U.S. Navy Seals Lead and Win* by Jocko Willink and Leif Babin. The concept of extreme ownership became foundational in my career.

You take full credit for your personal success and rely on yourself to achieve it. Likewise, you take responsibility for your mistakes and rely only on yourself to resolve them. Self-rescue, no one is coming.

Daily practice: Learn to take responsibility by adhering to the following practices:

- Keep your commitments and promises. This is key for gaining the trust and respect of others but, more importantly, fostering your own self-respect and integrity.

- Don't blame others or make excuses. This is just a waste of time and won't resolve an issue or fix a problem. Even if others are to blame, negativity ultimately affects your success. Consider yourself responsible and *work the problem* to a solution.

- Take responsibility for your words. Be sincere and honest at all times. Take responsibility for your thoughts and feelings as well. Express your emotions in healthy, inoffensive ways and try to keep your thoughts positive.

- Don't take things personally. You have a vision to pursue and greatness to attain. Don't mire yourself in trivial quarrels and feuds. Don't hold grudges and be willing to just move on.

- Celebrate your wins. Never forget to take responsibility for your brilliant successes. Be proud of your work.

4. Reconcile with your past

Ruminating about past mistakes, failures, and negative experiences is one of the key obstacles to achieving greatness. For some people, it's a key obstacle to any real success or advancement. Dwelling on the past is when you regularly revisit negative situations and experiences that happened in your life. You run these scenarios in your head, fueling emotions of guilt, shame, bitterness, and resentment. These emotions diminish self-worth, optimism, and motivation like nothing else.

As you can guess, a high achiever never looks back but always forward. They're totally reconciled with themselves and with their past. That's what you need to do as well.

Daily practice: If your past is haunting you, you need to understand why and reconcile with it. There are several options you can practice daily to ensure that the past stays in the past where it belongs.

- Refocus yourself immediately when you find your mind drifting back in time. Prepare a list of short activities that you can engage in to distract yourself and boost your mood. This could include listening to music, meditating for 10 minutes, going for a short run, calling up a friend to chat, etc. Make sure to choose activities that uplift and relax you.

- Practice mindfulness exercises. Mindfulness is a powerful tool that trains your mind to stay present in the here and now. Mindfulness exercises are simple and enjoyable. They'll gradually wire your brain to dwell less on the past and remain focused on the present. A quick web search will come up with a large variety of mindfulness exercises to choose from.

- Forgive yourself. Take the time for honest self-reflection. Acknowledge how your negative emotions are preventing you from living life to the fullest. Acknowledge your mistakes and failures and understand that you've learned from them and that they've made you stronger. Finally, make the heartfelt commitment to release those emotions and forgive yourself.

- Apply the same method to forgive others as well. Bearing grudges isn't going to change what happened. Releasing and forgiving others will liberate you from some very crippling emotions. If they do not help or support you then they hinder you. Forgive and move on.

- Choose to control what you can. You can't control the past or travel back to it, though if you could it would require 1.21 GWh. The same goes for the future, but you can choose to control what you have in the present to shape a great future. Ask yourself each day: what can I control today that will bring me one step closer to my vision? Then take action!

5. Stay alert for opportunities

Your career or life situation may be perfectly aligned with your vision. You're happy in your job or marriage or perfectly satisfied with your present circumstances as they are. You want to work with what you have in order to bring out the high achiever in you. Contrarily, you may not be satisfied with where you are now because you feel stifled or stagnant and realize that you'll never soar to greatness in your present situation.

In both cases, you need to stay alert for opportunities. In the first scenario, your search will be for opportunities that supercharge your success and achievement even more. In the second, you need to seek opportunities to change your status quo and align yourself with your purpose. Opportunities may make us uncomfortable because it forces us into the unknown but that is where growth happens. Take the step.

Daily practice: Stay alert for opportunities every day by putting the following into practice. Remember, even a tiny opportunity seized can lead to great things.

- Foster great relationships. Make sure you create and foster honest and open relationships with everyone in your life. Always try to give more than you receive. Your reward will be unlimited support and encouragement as well as some surprising opportunities.

- Network. Create a network of like-minded high achievers and work to continuously expand it. Sometimes, *it actually is* about who you know. There are few questions involving the forensic sciences that I can't quickly get an answer about through my professional network. Always give great value to your network peers. Go above and beyond when it comes to providing support, information, and contacts. You'll be rewarded ten-fold as these people eagerly try to reciprocate your help and sincerity.

- Never stop learning. High achievers are continuously learning and growing. Make it a habit to learn new skills, languages, or earn degrees and qualifications. They don't need to be related to your career or field. In fact, the more diverse your self-improvement is, the more unexpected opportunities may come your way.

6. Develop invincible persistence

As a high achiever, you need to adopt the NASA Apollo program mantra of "failure is not an option". This mindset breeds remarkable persistence. That's why high achievers are able to quickly bounce back from setbacks stronger than ever. That's also why they never give up.

Saddle up, light the engines, and go go go.

This quality is more commonly known as "grit". Like Sam Elliot bare-backing a rocket into the void of space "grit". A powerful combination of mental toughness, perseverance, resilience, and patience. Naturally, every high achiever possesses the quality of grit. Consider the research of Dr. Angela Duckworth on the theory of grit and its connection to success: her 2013 Ted Talk and her book *Grit: The Power of Passion and Perseverance.*

Daily practice: You can develop invincible persistence by tackling tough tasks and big projects:

- Be inspired by people with grit. Steve Jobs, Stephen Hawking, and George Washington Carver are just a few examples of people who persevered against incredible odds. Read their stories and be inspired by their superhuman persistence and their amazing achievements. Read about these people from time to time to maintain your own motivation and conviction that anything can be achieved.

- Raise your expectations. When faced with a challenging task, always expect it to be difficult to accomplish. This will mentally prepare you to put in the time, effort, and patience as well as to expect challenges along the way. Not every task to undertake will be labor intensive. In fact, you may breeze through with outstanding results. But raising the bar equips you with mental toughness in case things don't run smoothly.

- Give yourself enough time. In addition to raising the bar, try no to limit yourself with a tight timeframe. Plan well, think things through, and give the task the time it deserves to become a success.

- Know your 'why'. Find a way to relate the task at hand to your vision. Ask yourself why you're doing this. Is it to enable you to switch to a career more aligned with your vision? Is it to earn enough to start making your vision a reality? Having a strong 'why' will give you the persistence to overcome any hurdle and to never give up.

7. Be a pro at decision-making

High achievers never suffer from decision fatigue. This is one of the big gains you can expect to master and optimize. Decision fatigue means the perpetual inability to make timely and purposeful decisions. It's one of the most frustrating and stressful challenges you face on a day-to-day basis. It is the classic "where do you want to eat?" / "I don't know, where do you want to go?" dilemma. It's also a huge productivity and achievement-killer.

High achievers are pros at timely and effective decision-making. It's one of the core factors that enable them to keep the ball rolling, seize opportunities, outpace the competition, and skyrocket from one success to another. Make a decision and move on, make course corrections along the way.

Daily practice: Kick your habit of indecision with the following steps:

- Start small. Train yourself to make one or two quick decisions every day, ideally in less than a minute. This could be deciding what to wear to work, choosing between two food brands at the supermarket, or deciding what to order for lunch. Quickly weigh the options, and make a choice. This will speed up your thought process and decrease endless hesitation.

- Don't overload yourself with information. You don't need to pore over endless figures, statistics, or reports. Sometimes, information overload can lead to confusion and more hesitation. Decide beforehand what basic information you need to make the decision. For example, when buying a home appliance, you would need to have basic information such as pricing, functions, warranty, and customer reviews.

- Have a backup plan. Control risk factors by always having a plan of action in case the primary decision doesn't achieve the intended outcome. Having a backup or alternative plan decreases your fear of taking risks and ensures that negative outcomes can be quickly and efficiently resolved.

- Trust your intuition. Sometimes, your gut feeling is so strong that you know your subconscious mind is trying to tell you something. Don't ignore it! If your subconscious is sending you a barrage of red flags, you may need to rethink a decision or seek more information. If you get an extremely positive and uplifting feeling about something, go for it! This doesn't always happen with every decision you make but, when it does, pay attention to your intuition.

8. Dare to risk

The fear of taking risks is possibly the foremost reason that removes people from achieving their goals and maximizing their actual potential. High achievers don't exactly welcome risk with open arms, nor do they take hasty action despite their adventurous spirit. Not risk aversion, so much as a strategic consideration. They understand that there's a risk factor in virtually anything and refuse to let that hold them back. They also understand that big achievements sometimes require taking big risks. You can also empower yourself to be mentally prepared to take risks and overcome your fear. Bob Iger, CEO of the Walt Disney Company, explains the importance of risk taking very well in his book *The Ride of a Lifetime* as well as his Mater Class series. If you ever expect to gain distance, grow, or evolve you have to be willing to trust yourself and become a purposeful risk-taker.

"Who Dares Wins." -Motto of the British Special Air Service

Daily practice:

- Plan well. Consider all the various outcomes of a decision or action and plan well once you opt for it. Do your due diligence, gather the information you need, and consult qualified sources. Then, go ahead knowing you've done your best.

- Have a risk management plan. Assess the risks and create a risk management plan to quickly get back on track and minimize loss.

- Identify the 'why'. This is another case when knowing your 'why' is a powerful tool that gives you the courage to act. The more your 'why' is aligned to your vision and purpose, the more willing you'll be to give it your best despite the risks.

- Reframe your fear. The best way to overcome a fear is to reframe or modify it into something positive. When you're assessing risks, consider them as possible advantages. Rather than leading to a setback, or loss, consider the unseen opportunities that this could bring; this strives back to embodying the optimist.

9. Prioritize priorities

We all have priorities that we either tackle with daily to-do lists, as well as weekly or monthly schedules. The problem is that once we set those priorities, we think they're carved in stone. High achievers are keen on getting their priorities straight. The difference is that they're prepared for unexpected changes that could either change the order of priorities or require new ones altogether. Sometimes, the lowest priority on the list may become the highest.

Daily practice: Evaluate your priorities frequently to stay on track by practicing the following:

- Set short-term and long-term priorities. Separate your priorities into daily, weekly, and monthly ones. This makes it easier to revisit and reassess them as needed. Think both in the short and long term understanding the interplay of one into the other.

- Assess regularly. Revisit your priorities regularly to see if anything has changed. For example, review your daily priorities each morning to make sure you've scheduled tasks accordingly and whether a changed deadline requires putting one priority before the other. Do the same with your weekly and monthly goals, making modifications if needed.

- Be flexible. Develop the mindset of flexibility when it comes to scheduling and setting priorities. Many of us subconsciously think that a schedule needs to be stuck to no matter what. However, things are constantly changing, and unexpected situations arise almost every day. A flexible mindset will ensure a less stressful day and train you to quickly adapt to changes. *Adapt and Overcome.*

10. Focus on Health

The mindset of high achievers makes them naturally health conscious. They maintain their physical health by eating a nutritious diet, regular physical exercise (still striving for that one), and daily mental exercise. They make sure they get enough sleep and diligently de-stress. Sleep is one of the most critical aspects to master and fine tune.

Good sleep is dependent on the individual, but its importance is universal. Do not underestimate the compounding effects of your sleep health. On that note high achievers also understand the importance of strong mental health.

Great physical and mental health is essential for maintaining clarity, focus, and high energy levels as well as boosting all the other qualities of high achievement.

Daily practice: In addition to having a good health routine in place, here are a few suggestions for daily habits that'll can keep you feeling motivated:

- Stay hydrated. Drink water often, I'm not your mother so that's that.

- Take breaks. Keep your posture healthy and refresh your brain by taking breaks to stretch your legs and de-stress. A great idea is to take a 5-minute walk or run in place for a few minutes.

- Take a nap. Studies show that a deep 10-15 minute nap in the afternoon can be as refreshing as a full night's sleep. If you're feeling drained and have the luxury to do so, try this quick recharge.

- Stay active. Apart from your routine exercise program, find ways to stay active during the day. Walk rather than drive when you can, take the stairs, or walk to a local park during lunch breaks. The point is to be in motion and personify your mindset of productivity through constant physical momentum.

Conclusion

Designing Yourself

For these ten traits to become life-changing, you need to grow them into full-fledged habits. The only way to do that is with consistent and purposeful practice. Practicing them on and off is not going to develop the mindset of a super achiever. However, consistent daily practice will rewire your brain to slowly ingrain them in you. After applying them enough, they will become part of your personality and your character traits. You are designing now the person you want to be tomorrow.

You can start small with one or two that you practice daily until you find them coming naturally to you. Then add two more traits and so on until all of these core principles have become powerful habits and part of your new life as a high achiever. Finally, now that you've read this book, ask yourself again, what does a super-achiever have that you don't? Your answer should be a resounding 'absolutely nothing'.

Moral of the story: get your sh#t together and go do the impossible because the only person who can stop you is yourself. Design a plan of action and then execute it. Make course corrections along the way, but continue your optimistic momentum. It really is that simple, now go be a doer.

Afterword

Some of My Favorite Reads

1. *Extreme Ownership,* Authored By: Jocko Wilink and Leif Babin
2. *The Ride of a Lifetime: Lessons Learned from 15 Years as CEO of the Walt Disney Company,* Authored by Robert Iger
3. *Steve Jobs,* Authored by Walter Isaacson
4. *How to Be Like Walt: Capturing the Disney Magic Every Day of Your Life,* Authored by Pat Williams
5. *The 4-Hour Workweek,* Authored by Timothy Ferriss
6. *American Moonshot: John F. Kennedy and the Great Space Race,* Authored by Douglas Brinkley
7. *Elon Musk: Tesla, SpaceX, and the Quest for a Fantastic Future,* Authored by Ashlee Vance

About Author

Zack Kowalske is an award-winning Crime Scene Detective, Forensic Science PhD Researcher, nationally recognized Bloodstain Pattern Analysis expert, and space nerd. He lectures on issues of crime scene investigations and reconstruction, the future of forensic science, investigator trauma, and more. His presentations and media appearances include as a CSI expert on the Investigation Discovery Channel, interviews with several podcasts, and regular international conference and University engagements. He has been featured in Forensic Magazine and is a recipient of the Dr. William Bass Award for Outstanding Achievement in the Field of Forensic Investigations. In 2022, he became the first Forensic Science Researcher to study the concept of bloodstains in a Space or Microgravity environment, truly believing in the practice that no idea is too big or out of reach.

in linkedin.com/in/zackkowalske/

https://twitter.com/ForensicZack

instagram.com/forensicgeek/

www.ingramcontent.com/pod-product-compliance
Lightning Source LLC
Chambersburg PA
CBHW071123240526
45465CB00023B/797